Women Empowerment

Speak it Until You See it!

Women Empowerment

Speak it Until You See it!

Ebony Alexander-Knights

Cover Design by Erika Alexander

www.erikaolivia.com

I would like to thank my wonderful daughter Angie and supporting husband Rupert Knights, my strong and beautiful mother Verna and beautiful twin sister Erika, my good friend and sister Latoya Hull, Vision Strategist Neema Selah, sweet Mother-in-law Maricella and Bishop Hezekiah Walker who has encouraged me through out the years to put God first and to walk in Faith.

Contents

Your Words Are Powerful, So Use Them Wisely

Do you know you have the power to speak what you want to see in your life into existence? Do you understand that your words can produce great results? First, before we go any further into what you want, let's go over the following:

1. Make sure that what ever you do or go after is truly God's will for your life.
2. You must have faith in order to go after it.
3. Speak it until you see it!

I will go over these steps later in this book.

If you read the first few verses of Genesis Chapter 1 verse 1-3, it says something very interesting. It states, *"In the beginning God created the heavens and the earth. The earth was without form, and void; and darkness was upon the face of the deep. And the spirit of God was hovering over the face of the waters. And God said, "Let there be light;" and there was light."*

Did you get that? Go back to Genesis 1:3

Then God **said,** "Let there be light, and **there was light**."

I want you to take a moment as you ponder on that scripture. Now jump with me to verse 26 where it states, "Then God said, *"Let us make man in **our image**, according to our likeness."* Then verse 28 states, *"And God blessed them, and God said to them be fruitful and multiply; fill the earth and subdue it; have dominion over the fish of the sea, over the birds of the air, and over every living thing that moves on the earth."*

Not only did God say something and it happened, he made us in his image. Wait! Just think about that for a moment. HE MADE US IN HIS IMAGE. Now it goes on to say that we are to be fruitful and multiply. If you are a child of God and you are made in his image, could it be that you too can speak a word and see it come to pass too?

Words are so powerful! Actually, according to Proverbs 18:20, *"Death and life are in the power of the tongue; and they that love it shall eat the fruit thereof."* Think about that statement for a moment.

2

Your words alone can create positive results or negative ones in your life because your words are truly powerful. So your goal is to speak life. Speak your purpose so you can see your dreams come to pass.

Your Words are Powerful

So use it to promote good, life, joy, peace,
authority and abundance!

Figuring Out Your Purpose

For years I often tried to figure out what my purpose was and what was God's will for my life. I absolutely hated reading books that tell you to walk in your purpose but gave you no real direction. I've heard several speeches about walking in your purpose, but I wanted the speaker to just tell me what exactly my purpose is.

Have you ever felt that way? (Just tell me so I can do it) However I realized I had to figure it out for myself. Sometimes that's the best way because when you do, you are not going by what somebody else feels your purpose is, but you are going by what you know your purpose is.

Well, I finally figured it out. It's that part of you that you are naturally good at, it's an area where if you didn't have to think about bills, school, fear or anything else you would do it this very moment with great confidence, and yes, naturally. It's that thing you would probably do for free, but still feel fulfilled. Let me just give you a little preview of how I figured it out.

I went to college because as a child I wanted to be a Veterinarian. I absolutely loved animals. I would even pick up stray or injured dogs off the street and bring them home and take care of them. Although my mom did not quite agree with this, or of that really being my field, I still decided to go to college to become a Veterinarian.

After the daunting work in college with more paper work than hands on skills, I got a job during the school break at a Veterinarians office. Of course I was so excited until I realized what I was going to be paid (minimum wage) not including the long commute to get to the job. But to make a long story short, after two weeks of working at the Vet's office, I realized I did not have enough guts to put animals to sleep among the other extra duties they wanted me to do.

I realized that that was not the field for me. After two years of school, I had to change my major. I later had to find various jobs. I even attended a technical school focusing on health care. I loved helping people, so it was sure to work. After searching for a job in that field for a few years, I realized I had to stop to figure out what I was really supposed to do with my life.

I needed a job, but most importantly, I wanted to know what God's will was for my life so I could finally walk in it. I really had to think about what direction I was headed and what is the true career for me. One day, when I was feeling discouraged looking for work, a lady asked me what I liked to do. I told her I enjoyed helping people. But then I realized that just knowing that alone was not enough.

I had to figure out what is my specific area. In other words, you have to pin point it, so it will be plain and clear to you, that way you can move on it.

The same lady then asked me if I ever had a job that I really enjoyed. I told her, "Yes, it was the first job I ever had, which was working at a Senior Center." That day was an eye opener for me and at that moment I felt strongly, "That's it!" God intervened and allowed me to speak to someone who just took the time to make me think.

It's Your Gift!

If I had looked back over my life and had been in tune with myself and creator, I would have known it long ago and not have ignored it. My first summer job at the age of fifteen I worked at a senior center. Never having any prior experience I became a big hit getting seniors who were in their 90's to dance and laugh again. I even made Bingo a big hit. But it took all of that schooling and jobs that turned me down to finally figure out what my purpose was. It's what I do naturally. Something that was innate, something I was not formally trained to do. Something that if I choose to be trained in that field, it will just enhance what is already there.

If I had even looked back further I would have realized I always had a great and special relationship with my grandmother. I was always making her laugh. It was also very easy to communicate with her. I remember how she used to take my sister and I to nursing homes as children to sing to the elderly. Looking back on that now, I can see how it all ties in. (Think about your early experiences).

 Look for your natural gifts. Find out what comes naturally to you and then ask yourself, "How does this make me feel?" Those of you who just figured it out, you too will say "Oh yes, that's it!" It will feel like a light bulb just came on.

You should feel passionate about your gift. You should feel good about your gift. You will feel a peace within you and you will also begin to recognize the positive impact it makes on others, and that too will be a confirmation to you.

Someone's No is God's Yes!

I remember when I finally got a job as an adult working with seniors. I was working as a Recreation Aide. In other words, I played table games, lead exercise sessions and transported residents to different floors and to special programs. Although I loved working with seniors, my salary was still not where I wanted it to be. Plus I felt like I could be doing more in my field. Surprisingly, a year later I got a call to work for the city. I thought "benefits, more money, I'll take it!" So I left my job as a Recreation Aide and took the position working for the city. After I started the new job, I quickly realized the position was not for me. I worked much harder, longer hours and I felt extremely stressed every time I went to work. I had veered off the path where my light was, not just as a Recreation Aide, but in the field of enhancing the lives of the elderly.

I felt miserable working at my city job. The problem was, I had focused on the money and so called benefits. There is nothing wrong with wanting more for your life financially, so to me I had to give myself that opportunity especially knowing I was a single mom at the time.

However it made me realize that if you're not walking in your purpose, your job will feel exactly what it is, "a Job!" and if it's a stressful job, the stress is not worth it. Although I appreciated having a job, after working those long stressful hours the check was really not all that. It was more money than my prior job, but believe me, I was paying for it.

It got so bad working at my new city job that I wished they would lay me off. Well guess what? They did lay me off. When I got the letter that I was being laid-off, an unexpected excitement came over me. A few of my co- workers got the notice as well. They felt so bad, even the ones who hated and complained about their job everyday, some of them were crying.

My supervisor sadly asked me what I was going to do. I proudly told her, "I am going after my true purpose." She surprisingly said, "Wow, you go girl!"

I thought about my purpose and of course I knew it was working with seniors, but I told myself I don't want to be the one playing dominoes and checkers anymore. I want to be the one who is in charge; I wanted to have a say in the type of programs and activities being offered. That summer, I went on the internet, emailed my resume, and put my feet to action.

I traveled to various senior facilities. I came to the conclusion that I wanted to have a managerial position working with seniors and I knew I wanted to work within the Recreation department. I went to many senior centers and nursing homes, except for the one I had previously worked at. Of course I would not want them to know I was laid-off.

However, no sooner than I had started, I started feeling a little discouraged because the position I was looking for stated, I had to have several years of supervisory or managerial skills, or I had to have a Bachelors degree, or I had to have a certificate in Recreation Therapy. Seeing this and hearing that, really started to get me down. However I really felt deep down inside that that was what God was calling me to do. So I had to encourage myself and put my faith in action. I remembered a message my Pastor preached one Sunday called "How Bad

Do You Want It." I had to replay that in my mind as I sent my resume out.

Here's the test, I had to speak it until I saw it and move on it. Everyday I started telling myself. "I am a supervisor in the Recreation department. I work close to home and I love my job." I even said what my job responsibilities were, not to mention my salary, days and hours.

I also started writing it down and I stopped talking on the phone and telling people what I was doing. Everyday at home I would just speak my position and I also got biblical scriptures to back me up. Such as:

Proverbs 3: 5-6 *"Trust in the lord with all your heart and lean not unto your own understanding, in all thy ways acknowledges him, and he shall direct your path."*

Matthew 7:7 *"Ask and it shall be given to you; seek and you will find; knock and it will be opened."*

James 2:17- *"Faith without out works is dead."*

Luke 1:37 *"For with God nothing shall be impossible."*

John 14:14 – *"If you ask anything in my name I will do it."*

I quoted these scriptures all the time and I spoke the position I wanted out loud, even when I felt discouraged. One afternoon I was sleeping and I got a phone call. I checked my voice mail and there was a message that stated "Hi my name is _____ this message is for Ebony, the Assistant Director of the Recreation department is leaving and I heard so many good things about you and I would like you to come in for an interview."

When I heard that message I jumped out of bed and started praying and thanking God in advance for the position. I prepared myself for the interview and I even had new ideas ready to present.

Did you realize something? I stepped out in faith and put action to my talk (gave out my resume). But here's where the divine intervention happened. I got the call from the place I never sent my resume.

My old job that I left for a new position, called me back. What makes this even more interesting is that when I left that job, I did not stay in contact with any of my former co-workers and to top that, two days later after that first phone call another company called me to come in for an interview to work as a part time Dance Teacher.

Furthermore, on the initial interview at the nursing home, when we got to the part about the days and hours, I informed the Director that I will be working as a Dance Teacher two days a week. (This was faith talking ladies!) before I got either of the positions.

Talk about courage to speak that out of my mouth on an interview I've been waiting to get for so long. And guess what? I was hired for both jobs and was able to work five days a week and leave two days early to work with students as a Dance Teacher. I got two jobs in the same month. God is good. It's like he shows up just when you feel like you have done all you can or when you feel He's forgotten all about you.

Receiving that phone call and getting the position was confirmation to me that God heard my prayer, seen me put faith into action and most importantly it showed me that the thing I felt so strongly about was what he wanted me to do. It revealed to me the position I wanted was the right one. Contrary to what was around me, what I saw, heard or sometimes felt, I still had to apply faith.

I wrote down my goals and what I wanted. I had to trust God and speak it into existence. And yes even the responsibilities I listed became reality. My job is also close to home, I even got the salary I requested. Remember the power is in your tongue.

Listen to faith messages, put your foot to action and re-direct your thinking to line up to the greatness that is within you.

Believe in yourself and trust God that he can do the impossible and use you to do it. Also, know that if you are trying and doing all that you can and you don't see any results, check your faith to see if your faith is intact. Check the position you are applying for. Also could it be that you are really suppose to start your own business? Could it be your creator wants you to create your own career?

So many of us have gifts and talents that we are not using (i.e. cooking, dancing, organizing events, graphic arts and design etc.) and we are waiting for someone else to open the door.

Maybe it's time for you to open up your own door. If God instilled the vision in you and you have a desire to start your own, learn what you need to do and go after it!

Maybe it's time for you to open up your own door. Learn what you need to do and go after it!!!

9 Steps To Remember

1. Pray and ask God what is your true purpose and to show you.

2. Think about what you do well naturally

3. Write down your vision - Check out Habakkuk Chap. 2: 2.

4. Ask yourself "What would I do for free?"

5. Don't tell everyone your dream-block haters and unbelievers right now!

6. Shut off the television for much more than one day, take time for you and your thoughts until you make your dreams become reality (by doing this you are blocking distraction and channeling your time on your purpose).

7. Apply faith and believe in yourself even if nobody else does.

8. Get biblical scripture to back you up.

9. Oh yes, you know it, speak it until you see it!

Get the Vision

Create the Steps
You need to take.

Write it down

Strategize

Speak it

and

Move!!!

These are some of my personal affirmations that I enjoy speaking.

))) *I have the right connections and everything I need to be successful. I represent success!*

))) *I am happy, healthy and wealthy and my family is happy, healthy and wealthy too.*

Positive Affirmations

))) _I love what I do_

))) _I love my business and money is flowing!_

))) *I am truly making a difference in the lives of others and I am proud of my self.*

Positive Affirmations

))) *I am walking in my purpose and I am loving it!*

))) *My faith has increased as well as my walk with God. I recognize the blessing in every area of my life and I recognize the area of change and I accept it.*

))) *My determination and faith has produced great results and I am finally reaping the benefits.*

You can create your own inspiring affirmations; this is truly a great exercise. The more you do it the more you'll believe it, the more you believe it, the sooner you'll see it!

Afterword

Thank you so much for reading this book. There are more books to come. Check out my book called Single "Yes" But Desperate "No" (Unleashing the Power within You.)

If you are a young adult trying to figure out your purpose or you are preparing for college, I recommend volunteering a minimal of two weeks to three months, or even becoming an intern before you enter college. This will give you a little experience and confirm to you if the career you are pursuing, is the right choice for you.

I truly wish you all the best. Enjoy your journey. When you finally move in your purpose, it will push you, drive you, challenge you, bring the best out of you and surprisingly show you all the greatness that has been held inside for so long.

About the Author

Ebony Alexander-Knights and her husband Rupert Knights are a part of an organization called "Powerful Pioneers, Inc." Their goal is to empower youths and adults by offering various workshops such as dance, vegetarian cooking classes, and exercise and health presentations. Their mission is to spark vision, inspire faith and mobilize communities, as well as bridge the gap between the young and old.

Ebony is also a Choreographer, Author and Play Writer. Her passion is to enhance the lives of seniors, women and young adults through women empowerment workshops, dance, performance and play production.

She enjoys motivating and inspiring the young and old to go after their dreams and while doing so, hopes we too would give back our gifts, love and talents to others.

If you are interested in booking Ebony Alexander-Knights for community events/workshops or would like to purchase or order any books, you can contact her at the following address below:

Website: Powerfulpioneers.org

Email:humblelionessdm@gmail.com

Made in the USA
Charleston, SC
10 November 2016